A Remarkable Punctuation Family

Peter Period

Written by Barbara Cooper
Illustrated by Maggie Raynor

GARETH**STEVENS**
PUBLISHING
A World Almanac Education Group Company

Please visit our web site at: **www.garethstevens.com**
For a free color catalog describing Gareth Stevens Publishing's
list of high-quality books and multimedia programs, call
1-800-542-2595 (USA) or 1-800-387-3178 (Canada).

Library of Congress Cataloging-in-Publication Data

Cooper, Barbara, 1929-
    [Fergus Full Stop]
    Peter Period / written by Barbara Cooper; illustrated by Maggie
Raynor. — North American ed.
        p. cm. — (Meet the Puncs: A remarkable punctuation family)
    Summary: Introduces the use of the period through the story of Peter, a
member of the Punc family who has always been good at making things stop.
    ISBN-13: 978-0-8368-4227-2 (lib. bdg.)
    ISBN-10: 0-8368-4227-8 (lib. bdg.)
    [1. English language—Punctuation—Fiction.] I. Raynor, Maggie, 1946- , ill.
II. Title.
PZ7.C78467Pe   2004
[E]—dc22   2004045216

This North American edition first published in 2005 by
Gareth Stevens Publishing
A Weekly Reader Company
200 First Stamford Place
Stamford, CT 06912 USA

This U.S. edition copyright © 2005 by Gareth Stevens, Inc. Original edition
copyright © 2003 by Compass Books Ltd., UK. First published in 2003 as
(The Puncs) an adventure in punctuation: Fergus Full Stop by Compass Books Ltd.

Designed and produced by Allegra Publishing Ltd., London
Gareth Stevens editor: Dorothy L. Gibbs
Gareth Stevens art direction: Tammy West

Printed in the United States of America

2 3 4 5 6 7 8 9 10 09 08 07

Peter Period

is a V ● I ● P ● (Very
Important Punc) ●

His job is to keep
words and sentences
and the other Puncs
in order ●

Peter is round and fat,
but he is very fit ●
He has to be ●   He works
for the Punc Police ●

Peter is also a member of the
P ● D ● D ● T ● (Punc Daredevil
Display Team) ●

People say that Peter's ancestors were some of the first Puncs in history ● They were the very first Puncs to sail the seas and settle among different languages ●

Peter is proud of his ancestors ●
They were bold and strong ●
Wherever they went, they put things
in order ● They made words become
sentences and could bring them to
a STOP ● These Puncs really
knew how to stop trouble ●

When Peter was only a few months old, it was clear that, when he grew up, he, too, would be able to make things STOP.

When his mother tried to feed him spinach and other things he didn't like, Peter pushed the spoon away with his strong hand •

His mother then knew it was time
to STOP.

At school, Peter's teachers found him very helpful ● Whenever Peter saw boys fighting on the playground, he would rush in with his hands rolled into fists ●

"Stop that," he would shout in his gruff voice ●

Peter's voice was so strong and so powerful that the fighting would stop immediately ●

11

When he was older, Peter started going to the gym four times a week • He wanted to be even stronger, so he could join the Punc Police •

First, Peter did push-ups •
Push up • STOP •
Count to 10 • Down •

Then, he lifted dumbbells •

Lift • STOP • Hold • Down •

Peter quickly became the Puncs' top weight lifter •

13

Now, Peter is on the Punc Police force •
When he is on duty, he just raises
his hand to bring cars, vans,
motorbikes, and bicycles
instantly to a halt, which
is the same as a **STOP** •

Stop•

When he has to jot down quick notes, Peter has a useful way of shortening words ● He simply stops them ●

Wed ● Sept ● 1
3:40 p ● m ●
Saw g ● p ● ; i ● e ● , guilty party, parking white van on double line outside P ● T ● H ● (Punc Town Hall) ●
Vehicle (Lic ● No ● W176BAD) was i ● b ● c ● (in bad condition), e ● g ● broken headlight, 2 bald tires, etc ●

When Peter is not on
duty, he plays soccer ●
He is a member of the
P ● P ● S ● C ● (Punc
Professional Soccer Club) ●

Peter is a first-class goalie ●
His dives and leaps to stop
the ball from going
into the net ●

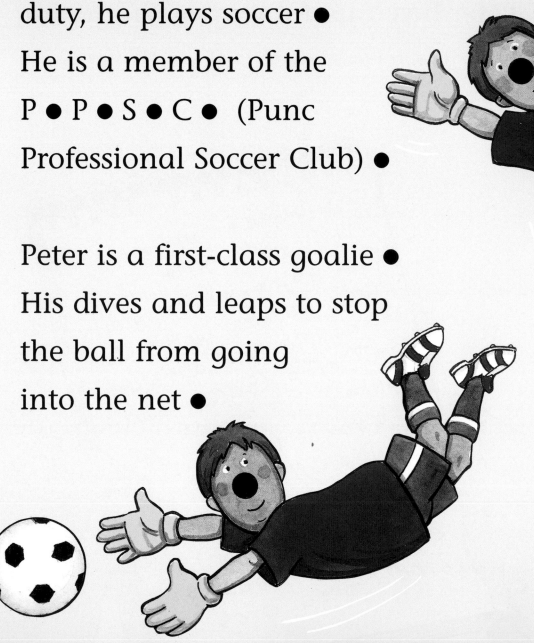

When spectators see that Peter is the goalie, it stops them from shouting rude words or throwing things onto the soccer field ●

Peter's mother, Penny, is a crossing guard ● She stops traffic so that children can cross the street ● Her job is to keep the children safe, so she does not let them misbehave ●

"STOP that,"

she scolds them sternly ●

Peter's father, Percival, is a security guard at a factory ● He stops visitors and asks to see their passes before he raises the gate to let them in ●

He also uses a stopwatch to keep track
of the times people go in and out ●

Peter's brother, Patrick, is also on a police force ● He is in the P ● M ● P ● (Punc Mounted Police) ● Riding his fearless horse, Stopper, Patrick easily catches up with troublemakers and brings their mischief to a STOP ●

Peter's Canadian cousin, Paul, and Paul's wife, Patsy, both work for the P ● P ● S ● (Punc Park Services) ● They stop park visitors and campers from feeding the wild animals and starting fires ●

Patsy is originally from England ●   Before she married Paul, her family name was Full Stop ● Patsy's father, Fergus Full Stop, is a famous British bobby ●

Peter tries to be friendly as well as firm, but one Punc really makes him angry ● It is Chris Comma ● Chris is always getting in Peter's way ● Peter likes to end sentences ●

STOP and think.

You will quickly see why Peter Period is a V. I. P. (Very Important Punc).

1. He stops words from wandering.
2. He brings sentences to a STOP.
3. He shortens words to save space.
4. He is useful for making lists, like this one.
5. Without him, Emma Exclamation Point and Quincy Question Mark would have something missing.
6. He is the only Punc that can bring this book, or any other, to an end.

Peter's Checklist

- Every sentence ends with a period, unless the sentence is a question (which ends with a question mark) or an exclamation (which ends with an exclamation point):
  Peter is very fit.
  Is that goalie Peter Period?
  Look out! Here comes Pete!

- Although not required, periods can be useful in writing short notes:
  Traffic duty. Go to gym.
  Repair motorcycle.
  Lunchtime. Call Mom.

- Use periods when you write your initials (the first letter in each of your names):
  P. P. (Peter Period)

- Use periods after titles before names:
  Mr. and Mrs. Paul Period
  Dr. Puncson

- Use periods to shorten long names:
  P. P. S. C. (Punc Professional Soccer Club). Shortened names (acronyms) are often easier to remember and are always quicker to write.

- Periods are also used to shorten words, forming abbreviations:
  e.g. (for example)
  i.e. (that is; in other words)
  etc. (et cetera; and so on)

- Periods can be used after numbers or letters when you are writing a list:
  1. Get up
  2. Get dressed
  3. Have breakfast

- Periods can help show whether the time is morning or afternoon:
  7:00 a.m.
  5:30 p.m.

- Three periods in a row (ellipsis) show that words have been left out:
  Chris Comma goes on, and on, and on, and on . . .

- Decimal numbers need periods. (These periods are called decimal points.):
  12.5 + 15.3 = 27.8

- Periods are needed in an E-mail address:
  peter.period@puncmail.com